It's 10:31 Somewhere © 2023

Karen Conway

Presentation by *BookLeaf Publishing*

Web: www.bookleafpub.com

E-mail: info@bookleafpub.com

ISBN: 9789358734119

First edition 2023

DEDICATION

To Bob, who lead me here and to Victoria and
Nicholas who saved me.

ACKNOWLEDGEMENT

"I hope you're ready, because amazing things are about to start happening for you." This was the quote that Karen saw online while trying to decide whether or not to embark on this endeavor. Feeling a spark of life again, she quickly took a screenshot of the quote and, later, noticed the time on the screenshot was 10:31...her late husband's birthday. Taking this as a sign from him, she started writing.

Still Here

I can barely perceive your voice, but sense your
essence near,
Visiting from the other side, proclaiming you're
still here,
I am aware of it in the morning, as I dread the
day ahead,
I can feel it while I brush my teeth and while I
make our bed.

Your fiery, blazing presence lights the blackness
of the night,
Each memory of your humor erases the memory
of each fight,
And in the flicker of a moment, when I permit
myself to laugh,
The refreshing burst of sanity is quickly cut in
half.

One day I felt that heavy sinking, and took it as
my cue,
To build a life of wonder, that I'll forever owe to
you.
The seeds you so unknowingly planted in my
mind,
Blossomed into whispers of "seek and you shall
find."

And every time I take a chance, and every time I
stand,
Every time I leap off the edge, I know I'll safely
land.
For every time I doubt the next step that I must
take,
I feel you there nudging me toward the move
that I must make.

I do not hesitate to say you're right here next to
me,
In my bones, I recognize you with every sign I
see.
And I'll keep "livin' the dream," just like I
promised you,
And I'll be sure to "go big or go home" just like
I know you'd always do.

I followed you through the valley of the shadow
of death,
Then you sighed, "it's not your time," and I
caught another breath.
I question if it happened; I wonder if it's true,
A shock so very violent, yet I'm still here…

      …and so are you.

As our children live their milestones, and I'm
the only one they see,

I'll save a seat for you, so you can cheer with
me.
'Cause from now until the day I die, in
everything I do,
I'll see those numbers or hear that song and
know in my soul it's you.

Familiar Ceiling

Sleepless, Springtime night,
Youthful laughter flowing from an open window,
And a suspicious dog thundering in the distance at
a slowly creeping car.

Invisible, dancing breeze,
Borrowing dinner's aroma to lay at every
windowsill,
As the last of the garbage cans loudly scrapes its
way back into the garage.

Vigilant, attentive feline,
Turning the room into a pinball machine,
Zipping after an invisible energy from another
dimension.

Sudden rush of panic,
Hearing every creek and moan of the walls,
Turning to my right, only to see the empty pillow
reminding me I'm alone.

Noisy, muddy brain,
Enveloped in the drowsy blue TV glow,
Unblinking eyes staring at a twirling fan on a
familiar ceiling.

No dreaming for me tonight

A New Life

Misty sky, still sleepy-eyed, and resurrected
beams of light,
Burn holes across my face, while my alarm
picks a screeching fight.
If only I was still dreaming, I'd think, as my feet
heavily hit the floor,
The torment and toil and torture; they all exist
no more.

Today there is no thunder, no dreariness, no
haze.
Today there's no uneasiness; my head's not in a
daze.
I willingly introduce myself to the hours that lay
ahead
What wondrous events await me once I explode
right out of bed?

Beautiful bright and shining sun grins down
from the noon sky.
Never again will I submit to all the restrictions
of the lie.
I'd rather return to what I'd forgotten, but
remember once again,

I'd rather die a thousand deaths than punish
myself 'till the end.

I yearn for this day to last forever; I wish every
eye could see,
You don't need to ask permission; all your
desires can be.
The pink and orange sun will soon surrender to
the glowing moon.
Reluctantly I'll say goodnight, but the night has
come too soon.

Carpet footprints

Back to the way of life I know,
Trudging through the motions,
Existing to survive but not really to live.

Back to trying to sleep
and sleeping to try
and trying to laugh so hard I cry.

Faded memories of Monday
Trickle back
Through the little cracks in my brain
I forgot to plug up with broken pieces of
paradise.

Back to footprints on the carpet and not the
sand,
And only one Saturday night a week,
The time of my life
Must hibernate, until next time.

Back to the performing arts,
But I know I'll miss
Living life to really live
and not just exist.

Anxiety

A billion times she lay paralyzed with a tornado
in her brain,
And a dumbbell in her gut,
With notions far from sane.

A million times she dropped her weary feet to
the ground,
And stood with a dizzy gait,
Shackled, enslaved, bound.

A hundred times she saw a reflection she didn't
know,
So she stopped being surprised
And started laying low.

Every single lie that her mind made her believe,
Became a new religion,
A new conviction, a new creed.

No possibility of knowing just how to steer,
Through the overwhelming angst
And unrelenting fear.

A hundred times before, her thoughts were in a
race,

Toward an imaginary finish line
Then gone without a trace.

A million pills to shield her from the truth she
had to know,
To ever make a difference,
To ever learn and grow.

A billion mouths still screaming, that this is just
the deal,
But she recognizes the illusion,
And her heart, it knows what's real.

No more will she lay paralyzed with a tornado in
her brain,
Truth is stronger than this torment,
She's now fiercer than the pain.

Autumn

Floating in the colors of the Autumn of my life,
I know what I need to do,
As I muster the last of my strength to stab an
obscure fear
Through the heart.

Twirling through the apple reds and pumpkin
oranges,
Through the brown greens and yellow
Perishing leaves.

Weeping in the cinnamon spice Halloween
night,
For more reasons than one.
Afraid to plunge that jagged edge into all of the
Would-a, could-a, should-a's
That have always owned my might.

Even when my life was Springtime, and I didn't
know what I didn't know,
And I could smell the rain before it fell,
Drifting off to sleep, faded murky grown-up talk
Growing softer as I'm glided up the stairs to bed
And the safe, soft, subtle protection of my
teddy-bear lamp.

Then I was dancing through a summer heaven.
Glimpses of a beautiful forever that sadly would
never come,
but I didn't know that at the time.
While falling through the bluest sky I ever saw
into the wonderland below.

Even then…I couldn't see it.

Finally my season is here and Autumn hints it's
getting late,
With each lightning bolt it crashes into my
shield.
Now I'm armed with awareness and I'm awake.
Winter will surely reminisce of the autumn night
I said no more.

Awakening

Oh how I've taken Your name in vain,
In the midst of anger or in the depths of pain,
So I'll honor and obey and drop to my knees,
Clasping my hands and waiting to see.

God I've wandered down all the wrong roads,
I've turned and twisted, but bore all the loads,
The fire and brimstone, the demons - the dead,
Would swallow me whole if they heard things
I've said.

My holiness displayed wherever darkness goes,
Making extra sure that everyone knows,
I'm one of the good ones, I do what I'm told,
The infinite guilt, I closely hold.

The jolt that gifted me limitless doubt,
Grabbed the floor and ripped it right out,
The familiar looked different as it crumbled and
died,
All the mouths that spoke truth, were the ones
that had lied.

I stood in amazement and gazed with such awe,

As the veil was slowly lifted and the pieces
started to fall,
Hindsight's perfection boasts its swanky song,
And I'm astonished that I could be that wrong.

In the name of the Father, I opened my eyes,
In the name of the Son, I broke off the ties,
It was worth all the torture, the anger and the
pains,
To break free from the ones that kept me in
chains.

The Wink

I fell in between the summer and floated past the
screams,
I lovingly gazed at Christmas and stumbled past
our dreams,
There were your eyes in front of me; I did not
dare blink,
Everything started that night, with some guts
and a wink.

Through the orchestra of the daytime and the
ballet of the night,
We laughed ourselves into the perfection of the
light,
And now when the weight of it reaches a new
high,
And I'm at the precipice of do or die,

When the rock and the hard place have all but
met,
When I can't remember all I learned to forget,
When the last of my inspiration goes to sleep,
And I can't figure out how to take that leap.

I'll take a step back, I'll breath and I'll think,
How everything changed with a little old wink.

"If nowhere I venture then nothing I'll gain,"
The words that my soul whispered to my brain.

On the night, last decade, when I first saw your face
A stranger, yet so familiar in that time and place.
I floated past the Wildwoods and drifted through the snow
I heard some "Trick or Treats" and caught a glimpse of Mexico.

Now I'm back here pacing, my heart about to sink.
But I remember the miracle of a smile and a wink.

Crooked Bush

The breeze sifts silently through the crooked
bush across the street.
The one I never noticed before,
And now it's all I can see.

It's so late that it's early and the speckles of the
sunlight
Set off the blissful songs of the birds.
The same songs I used to loathe.

Floating down the sidewalk bathed in the
bubbles of light,
Cleansed of the nightmares of yesterday,
The ones that shook me so brutally my eyes
opened.

For decades I told you what you wanted to hear,
For years I played by all of your rules,
Forcing my square life in your round reality.

The gentle buzz of the bee on the other side of
the screen,
Reminds me that there are many sounds I never
heard,
Many crooked bushes punching me in the face,

That I denied were even there.

But now I taste the summertime and hear music
in the
Flickering of the candle that smells like
magnolias.

But no one else notices the crooked bush again
today
As I snicker, alone.

Screaming

I whisper, but no one can hear me,
I speak softly, but everyone hums,
I raise my voice so maybe they'll listen,
I speak up - more chaotic it becomes.

My screaming voice drowned in a crowd
of different people with the same face.
Every one a mirror of the last,
Complacent in their comfortable place.

If I could just catch someone's eye,
If I could see inside their dreams,
Maybe then somebody would notice
That I'm still bellowing out my screams.

Drowsy, dreary, downhearted,
Stumbling through the endless night,
Begging someone to answer me,
I cannot keep up this fight.

Letters that go unopened,
Anguish you cannot hear,
Burning desperation,
Persistent, unyielding fear.

I notice a girl softly praying,
As her tears stream down to the floor.
She reminds me of myself in a way,
I tell her to cry no more.

She turns to me and stares,
Her eyes aglow and beaming,
"I have been trying to get your attention," she
says,
"But you were too busy screaming."

The Voice

There's a voice that speaks out to me,
And calms the wild moments in time,
When life swallows every good intention I had.

There's a voice my ears don't notice,
That swirls around my being
Lighting each cell as it dances by,
Gluing together broken shards of unkept
promises.

The same voice that scolds my boldness,
Will torch every sacred dream I've ever had,
Because I'm not good enough,
It's not realistic enough,
Or I'm not ready.

My brain fighting endless battles
with the one aware of it.

The voice is mine.

Watch Me

Life's finger on the trigger of a gun aimed at my
head,
A thousand feet of water my legs are forced to
tread,
The hours in the day are not nearly long enough,
The days in the week are too torturous and
tough.

Stumbling through the decades, I had no other
choice,
In trying not to drown, I misplaced my own
voice,
And in trying to please, I overlooked my own
strength,
For that pat on the head, I'd go to any length.

Finally one day I thought, "what if I try,
To stop treading water; live or die?"
They thought, in that instant, I would surely
drown,
But my mind was not lost, it had finally been
found.

The other side of "what if" is a thought most
can't bear,

And I was discouraged from looking, but I
didn't care.
So with a splash of faith I stopped kicking for a
while,
My feet felt the bottom and I stood with a smile.

Daydreams transformed into action, like water to
wine,
Believing to my core, in each and every sign.
Get busy living or you might as well die,
Get busy diving into that other side of why.

Because nothing changes, if everything's the
same,
Surrendering to security yields nothing but
blame.
Endless possibilities, everything is true,
The voice contesting it's real...is you.

Constant reassurances that I am going to be fine,
As long as I keep accepting walking the line.
They'll say I can't do it, I'm not brave I'm not
free,
I'll say look out, open your eyes,

       and watch me.

Reborn

Do not force upon me fear, for I've lived with it
for years.
Cannot trick me into sadness; almost drowned in
oceans of tears.
Life does not intimidate; I laugh with every
breath,
I'm not anxious about my time on Earth; I'm not
afraid of death.

I've danced with all those petty fears, long into
the night.
I've swam right through the fires of hell, despite
the grasp so tight.
I looked into the Devil's eyes and scowled right
through his moans.
I seized a horn as a souvenir and brought back
fire in my bones.

Once, I watched so helplessly while the flames
destroyed and seared.
I screamed in agonizing grief as the whole world
disappeared.
I looked around at the burnt scraps of the little
that remained,

Then from the ashes in my soul I rose against
the grain.

It charred to pieces my nervousness; it
cauterized my cries.
It scorched away trepidation and beamed out of
my eyes.
The Devil laughed so confidently, thinking it
would break me,
But the scorching fire meant to destroy, was the
very thing to make me.

So, when I feel those doubts creep in, I take a
breath and turn,
I glare upon my keepsake and the fire starts to
burn.
I withstood the voyage to Hell and back, I
earned the Devil's horn,
The day I stopped being afraid was the day I was
reborn.

When I Used to Know You

When I used to know you,
Before time turned upside down,
And before I needed the pain, just to know I was
still alive.

When you used to care,
Before I woke from the coma,
And before all was too much and nothing was
not enough.

When you used to call,
Before death snuck in,
And halved my life with a swift, sudden slash of
its blade.

When I used to know you,
Your shadow fell with mine,
And every echoed laughter gave birth to a new
memory.

When you used to know me,
I...didn't even know me,
And I was oblivious to the volcano that was yet
to erupt.

When I used to care,
My chest heaved with torture,
And my throat became the desert, having
screamed out all the rain.

When I used to know you,
I thought I'd know you still,
And never dreamed I'd only see you in old
pictures at the bottom of an attic box.

I called you all my soul's mates,
In another lifetime,
When I used to know you.

Just for Today

I'm quiet, but I'm not blind.
I see all you try to hide,
Even if I don't tell you.

I'm alone but I'm not lonely.
I busy myself with the whispers
Of all of my yesterdays.

I'm forgiving, but I don't forget.
Your every betrayal lends
Strength to my wisdom.

I can hear you but I'm not listening.
Every word another dagger
In each life experience that's brought me this far.

I'm still here, but there's not much left.
I was sold off in parts
As I willingly gave up more of me to build you
up.

I love you, but I'm almost empty.
I'll sacrifice all I have tomorrow, but…

Today, just today, I love me more.

The Day I Came Home Alone

On the day that I came home alone,
Reality wasn't real,
And I heard a voice here and there.
No way of telling, but I think it was mine.

I made all of the usual phone calls,
While we put a pot of coffee on,
And I stared at the clear hospital bag of your
clothes,
The very ones you just put on last night.

On the day I came home alone,
I realized I never came home at all.
I died with you, and I was a stranger in our
house.

I heard myself tell the children
that you weren't in pain anymore,
As I put your glasses in a drawer,
And feared I would forget your voice someday.

I learned the meaning of numb that day,
As I checked the clock and it dawned on me
We were laughing together this time yesterday.

I didn't know that muscles can just stop
working,
Or hearts can turn to stone,
But I certainly learned those things that day -
The day I came home alone.

Now

A lifetime is not much, in all of time
It's like a sentence in a novel
I used to read over and over again,
When I thought time could be frozen
And saved for later on
When I was ready to live.

As years are seconds in all of time,
And months are grains of sand on the beach,
Days laid trampled on the ground,
When youth was all I thought there'd ever be,
And it didn't dawn on me
That it wouldn't last forever.

As I am no one in all of time.
Generations forgotten,
As history becomes a whisper-down-lane
Until it's lost for good,
And we all end up living lies
That parade around as common knowledge.

As none of it really matters in all time,
And none of us know what we never knew.
Some wallow in yesterday's pain,
Or stock up for tomorrow's famine,

Lost in "should have" and "what if,"
While "now" lays dormant, lost in the corners of
our mind.

Saved

Would you believe me if I told you
That when the room faded into black,
And I was desperate to let go,
Your faces held me back.

Would you call me a liar if I said
I thought it must have been fate,
That my time was surely up,
But something made me wait.

You may think I'm making it up,
But you'll never know my mind
Told me to fade into the light
But my heart couldn't leave you behind.

And I know you'll think I dreamed it,
You'll think that it's not true,
That I fought to come back to the pain,
I fought to come back to you.

I knew I needed to save you
From life's cruel destiny,
Not knowing in the moment
That you wound up saving me.